MEETING JESUS AT THE TABLE

MEETING JESUS AT THE TABLE

A Lenten Study

CYNTHIA M. CAMPBELL
AND CHRISTINE COY FOHR

WITH ILLUSTRATIONS BY
KEVIN BURNS†

WJK WESTMINSTER JOHN KNOX PRESS
LOUISVILLE • KENTUCKY

First edition
Published by Westminster John Knox Press
Louisville, Kentucky

23 24 25 26 27 28 29 30 31 32—10 9 8 7 6 5 4 3 2 1

Book design by Erika Lundbom
Cover design by Marc Whitaker/MTWdesign.net

Library of Congress Cataloging-in-Publication Data

Names: Campbell, Cynthia McCall, author. | Fohr, Christine Coy, author. | Burns, Kevin, 1967-2022, illustrator.
Title: Meeting Jesus at the table : a Lenten study / Cynthia M. Campbell and Christine Coy Fohr ; with illustrations by Kevin Burns.
Description: First edition. | Louisville, Kentucky : Westminster John Knox Press, [2023] | Summary: "This unique resource for Lenten study links together disparate stories across all four Gospels to show patterns and themes in Jesus' table ministry, with illustrations that offer extra interest and appeal"— Provided by publisher.
Identifiers: LCCN 2022042459 (print) | LCCN 2022042460 (ebook) | ISBN 9780664267797 (paperback) | ISBN 9781646982943 (ebook)
Subjects: LCSH: Lent—Study and teaching. | Jesus Christ—Evangelistic methods. | Dinners and dining in the Bible.
Classification: LCC BV85 .C348 2023 (print) | LCC BV85 (ebook) | DDC 242/.34--dc23/eng/20221020
LC record available at https://lccn.loc.gov/2022042459
LC ebook record available at https://lccn.loc.gov/2022042460

With gratitude to my husband, Fred Holper,
who taught me how to minister at the Lord's Table
and how to be a better cook.
— Cynthia

With gratitude to my spouse and son,
Kimberlee and Brennen Burns,
who cared for and sustained me as my illness persisted
through the development of this book.
— Kevin†

For First Presbyterian Church
of Owensboro, Kentucky,
where I first saw Christ's Table come to life.
— Christine

CONTENTS

Introduction

COME TO THE TABLE

A Lenten Bible Study

Lent is a journey, the end of which is the death and resurrection of Christ. It is a season in which we are invited to reflect on the immensity of God's love made known in Jesus and his victory over sin, evil, and death. In Lent we are invited to recall what it means to be disciples, followers of Jesus, each and every day. In the last days of Jesus' life, he sat at a table sharing the Passover meal with his closest friends and connecting the ancient story of God's liberating power with himself. After the resurrection, Jesus' disciples began to gather regularly to break bread in his memory and to experience him in their midst. We do the same thing today. But the upper room was not the only time Jesus was at table or told stories about tables. In this study, we invite you to consider some of these table stories and to reflect on them as we come to the Lord's Table together in this Lenten season.

"This is the joyful feast of the people of God! People will come from north and south, and from east and west to sit at table in the kingdom of God."[1]

These words are often used to invite us to the Lord's Table. They call us to imagine that, when we gather for the Lord's Supper, we are part of something much bigger than our particular congregation or community. This is a Table that stretches around the world and across time. Regardless of the season of the church year or

1. Office of Theology and Worship for the Presbyterian Church (U.S.A.), *Book of Common Worship* (Louisville, KY: Westminster John Knox Press, 2018), 26.

the occasion of the service, this meal is one of celebration and joy. The meal we share at the Lord's Table is one in which a small amount of food provides deep nourishment for the soul. At this Table, there is always room for whoever shows up, and there is always enough for all to be fed. Breaking and sharing bread has been at the heart of Christian worship since the beginning and remains so today. Even though all Christians are not yet able to share the Lord's Supper together officially, the Table remains a symbol of our anticipated unity with one another and with Christ.

The New Testament doesn't tell us much about how the Lord's Supper was observed in the earliest church, but stories about tables are everywhere in the Gospels. Jesus tells stories about banquets, and he goes to a lot of dinner parties. He eats with religious leaders and shady characters. He feeds a hungry crowd and tells his followers to do the same. In this study, we invite you to explore some of the stories about Jesus and tables and, through them, to reflect on how tables shape our identity as followers of Christ.

Just as the Lord's Table stands at the center of Christian worship, so gathering with others to share a meal is at the heart of the human experience. Eating food sustains our bodies. Eating with others creates community and sustains our spirits. Feasting and the preparation and sharing of special foods is part of every religious tradition and most cultures as well. Many families have their own traditions about foods that are always eaten on certain occasions (chili on Christmas Eve or barbecue on the Fourth of July or that special dessert for each family member's birthday). Even though the church potluck supper is a thing of the past in many congregations, faith communities still find ways to combine food and fellowship.

For some people, however, eating is neither communal nor pleasurable. Those who live alone often struggle with mealtimes because they are occasions of loneliness rather than community. Many in this world, indeed many in our own communities, are "food insecure." They simply do not have adequate resources to provide food for themselves or their families. And even more people live in "food deserts," neighborhoods where fresh, nourishing produce and protein are nearly impossible to find. When food and eating become metaphors for God's reign, it is as much about justice as it is about spiritual nourishment.

We—Christine, Cynthia, and Kevin—have chosen the following Gospel readings because they represent a range of stories about food and feasting from the life and teaching of Jesus. The idea for this book was suggested by Christine, inspired by a sermon series conversation in an online group called Young Clergy Women International. Cynthia has written the meditations for chapters 1 and 2, 6 and 7 (Palm Sunday and Maundy Thursday). Christine has written chapters 3 through 5 and 8 (the meditation for Easter). Each meditation is introduced by a visual interpretation of that particular story by architect and biblical teacher Kevin Burns. You will find his own reflections on how the text sparked his imagination at the end of each chapter.

This study can be used in a variety of ways: for individual meditation or as a springboard for group study and conversation. There are questions for reflection and discussion at the end of each chapter to help you enter into and engage these stories with us, and a guide for church leaders in the back with suggestions for using this study as a sermon series and in other ministries of the congregation.

Lent is a season for deepened reflection on the meaning of Jesus' life and ministry, death and resurrection. It is also a time for us to reflect on what it means to be called to follow Jesus in our own lives individually and as communities of faith. We hope that these table stories draw you closer to Christ and to one another as the body of Christ and that you will always be able to recognize him in the breaking and sharing of bread.

Kevin Burns
Cynthia Campbell
Christine Coy Fohr

Chapter 1

DINING ALFRESCO

The Feeding of the Multitude

READ: MARK 6:30–44

And he said to them, "How many loaves have you? Go and see." When they had found out, they said, "Five, and two fish." Then he ordered them to get all the people to sit down in groups on the green grass. So they sat down in groups of hundreds and of fifties.

—Mark 6:38–40

HAVE YOU EVER BEEN HUNGRY? *REALLY* HUNGRY? I acknowledge that I am among those in this world who are incredibly privileged; perhaps you are too. I've occasionally had a growling stomach, but I have always known that I could and would, sooner or later, get enough to eat. I've never known life-threatening hunger for food. But I have been famished for hope, for courage, for companionship. Maybe you have too. Perhaps you have also experienced a deep and abiding hunger for meaning and purpose, for a second chance, a fresh start, for forgiveness, for love.

Stories about hunger and food are all over the Bible. As this study suggests, many of the most significant events in Jesus' ministry occur when he is at a dinner table. When the Bible tells stories about hunger or uses food and drink (bread and wine) as metaphors for God's presence, the backdrop is real hunger. The Bible emerged out of the lives of people who were often food insecure. Most of the people in Galilee in Jesus' day were one step away from hunger: one bad harvest, one season of warfare, one disaster or another. People were starving. No wonder food and eating became metaphors for God's providential care and promise.

There are a half-dozen incidents from the life of Jesus that are told by all four of the Gospels—and his birth isn't even one of them. The feeding of the multitude in the wilderness is; in fact, this story occurs six times, because Mark and Matthew tell essentially the same story twice (just with different numbers of attendees). Thus, our first story of Jesus "at table" isn't a table at all, but a picnic, and the crowd is huge. Behind it, of course, is another story of wilderness, hunger, and bread.

Drought, crop failure, and famine were the things that got the descendants of Abraham and Sarah to Egypt in the first place. Modern-day refugees from natural disasters cross borders in search of a way to make a living. In just the same way, the twelve sons of Jacob and their families migrated from the land of Canaan to Egypt in search of food and work. After generations in that land, the people of Israel found themselves enslaved to the Egyptians, but at least they had food. Then, Moses was sent to lead them from slavery to freedom. Once they escaped into the wilderness, the Israelites were free, but they were famished. Like hungry children everywhere, they complained: "You could have left us to die in Egypt. At least we would have had food to eat!"

God knew their hunger, just as God knew and heard and felt their suffering in slavery. And so, quail appeared in the evening, and in the morning there was white stuff on the ground that could be gathered and eaten. "What is it?" they asked, *Manhu?* in Hebrew, which becomes our word "manna" (Exod. 16:1–15). What is it? It is what it is. Bread from heaven. Bread in the wilderness. Food at the moment of greatest insecurity. Food that keeps body and soul together. The bread of life.

This story is told over and over again in the Hebrew Bible. It is sung in the Psalms and called to mind by the prophets. Deeply embedded in the memory and imagination of Jesus and all his ancestors, it clearly stands behind each story of the feeding of the multitude in the wilderness.

Every version begins the same way. A large crowd has followed Jesus out to a hillside away from the surrounding villages. They are there to hear him teach. They are drawn by what he says and by stories that invite them to a deeper, larger life with God. They are drawn as well by the things he does, especially his embrace of illness that turns into healing and restoration. Nearing the end of the day, they are still hungry, and Jesus knows that people need food—for both body and soul. The details in the stories vary, but from somewhere (from someone in the crowd or perhaps the disciples themselves) food is found: five loaves and two fish. In Jesus' hands and with his blessing, this meager meal feeds a multitude, and then the disciples collect the leftovers: twelve baskets of abundance.

The COVID pandemic taught us a lot about hunger. It reminded us that food isn't just about eating. A meal isn't merely consuming the calories needed to sustain life. Food is meant to be shared. Meals are things that bring people together and create relationships. On the one hand, those of you who live in families may have had more meals together than you have had in years. On the other hand, those who live alone experienced the profound absence of companionship—others with whom to share bread. After six months of eating all our meals in our apartment by ourselves, my husband and I formed a "pod" of safety with another couple who lives nearby. In the fall of 2020, we ate a few meals off tray tables outside on their patio. But the first time we shared a meal together inside at the dining room table, we were all in tears. It was truly the joyful feast of the people of God.

The pandemic also revealed to us that many people in the United States are one step away from food insecurity. When so much of the economy shut down in the spring and summer of 2020, people lined up at food distribution sites. Long lines of people in nice cars drove through church parking lots to get a couple bags of groceries. Especially with schools closed and free breakfasts and lunches gone, it turns out that lots of families in this nation live very close to the edge where food is concerned. For many in those lines, anxiety was compounded by shame. More than one person said, "We used to be people who bought extra food to take to food banks, and now here we are." Personally, I find this deeply troubling. In one of the richest nations on earth, it just doesn't seem right that so many people could be so close to being hungry. Surely, we can do better as a nation. Surely, we want to do better.

The research office of our denomination asked Presbyterians what they missed most about in-person worship. The most frequent response was "Communion." Eating a piece of bread and sipping a little wine at home just isn't the same, it turns out. We may not consume much food, but when we come to the Table at church, it is a real meal because it is shared with one another in the presence of the One who said, "I am the bread of life. Whoever comes to me will never be hungry, and whoever believes in me will never be thirsty" (John 6:35).

Lent is a season when many Christians practice some sort of fasting. Abstaining from food as a way of focusing one's attention on God is both an ancient and widespread practice. The roots of the Christian practice are in the worship of Israel, where fasting was often urged as a sign of the people's intention to return to God's ways and renew their promise to be God's covenant people. Fasting remains a part of Jewish worship, especially on Yom Kippur (the Day of Atonement). Many Muslims fast during the daytime for Ramadan, a month-long time of spiritual renewal and recommitment. For some Christians, the practice of fasting is a practice of self-denial that helps one identify with the suffering of Christ. Others see it as a way to recognize our sin and our need for God's mercy and forgiveness.

Fasting is neither a weight-loss program nor a way to punish ourselves through lack of food. In fact, fasting can take many forms. Some limit or abstain from certain foods (like meat or dairy, alcohol or desserts). Others fast by preparing one or more "simple" meals each week and setting aside the difference of the cost to be contributed to a hunger offering. Fasting may have nothing to do with food but rather focus on time. Some find it meaningful to limit their TV or social media use and instead to concentrate on reading Scripture, praying, or volunteering in the community.

Whatever form fasting may take as a practice during the season of Lent, it is a tangible way to reflect on the fact we do not live by bread alone. That is one of the themes that stands behind the stories of the feeding of the multitude. In the Gospels, as in the exodus story, the people are in the wilderness—a place of scarcity where neither food nor water can be taken for granted. In their time of need, God provides them with bread—a symbol for what sustains life each and every day. But manna in the wilderness is a day-to-day thing: the people can only gather enough food for *one day at a time* (except on the day before the Sabbath, so that they can rest from gathering). The dailiness of this is intended to remind the people that what is important here is not *what* they are eating but *who* provides it. We do not live only because of the food we eat. The deep nourishment we need comes from God, whose very Word is bread. Food that keeps body and soul together. The bread of life.

ARTIST'S REFLECTION

Feeding the multitude was clearly a fundamental and critical story for the early church. The context for the story is typically understood as a deserted place away from the cities and towns, out in nature. The event calls into question our devotion to the idea of scarcity and our unwillingness to look to the divine for the miracles of sharing and compassion, of trustworthiness and reliance on God and our community. The story also places the disciples as key characters with the obligation to exercise agency in determining the outcome. Jesus breaking bread is the pivotal image in every version of the story. The imagery draws us to the story of the Last Supper, and in the case of Luke's Gospel, to the Emmaus reveal. We are reminded that all the Gospel writers recognized the centrality of Jesus' role in engaging the memories and imagination of the participants, ultimately inspiring an atmosphere of sharing.

We too often bifurcate the spiritual and the secular in the modern world, limiting sacred experiences to what we enjoy in our churches and temples while everyday life goes on six days a week among our friends and coworkers. However, the Bible often invites us to merge these realities.

The scene of a large group of people sharing and eating together out in nature speaks to that sacred-ordinary reality for me. In my illustration, I imagined a park setting with people sitting on the ground in smaller groups, but with everyone very much aware of the larger community that surrounds them. The earth is the table here, and it is set for a great banquet with Jesus in the center breaking the bread. This metaphor challenges us to view our community as much larger than we are accustomed to thinking of it. If the earth is our table, what does it say about our understanding of community and diversity? How does this inform our understanding of the scarcity of resources? How does it speak to the miracle of God's love in our world? Too often we get hung up on how the miracle worked in this story of multiplying resources and we miss the real miracle of why an expanded table is made manifest and available to all.

QUESTIONS FOR REFLECTION

1. Read the six versions of this story in all the Gospels: Matthew 14:13–21; Matthew 15:32–39; Mark 6:30–44; Mark 8:1–9; Luke 9:10–17; and John 6:1–14. (If you are studying as a group, assign different people or small groups to read each.) What details are common across

versions and what details are unique? Do these differences matter to you?

2. The author suggests that the crowds who followed Jesus likely experienced food insecurity. How does that affect your understanding of the story? How does it affect your thinking to realize that there are likely people in your congregation experiencing food insecurity?

3. When have you experienced God's provision? Was it a surprising, miraculous type of situation, like manna from heaven, or something more commonplace?

4. How did the COVID-19 pandemic affect your communal dining experiences (both in terms of social events and Holy Communion)? Did eating alfresco take on new significance for you?

5. How do you balance abstention and abundance in your life? How can abstaining from something during Lent open your eyes to God's abundance?

6. How does this chapter's illustration speak to you in light of the themes discussed?

Chapter 2

THE WELCOME TABLE

"He Eats with Tax Collectors and Sinners!"

READ: MATTHEW 9:9–13

And as he sat at dinner in the house, many tax collectors and sinners came and were sitting with him and his disciples. When the Pharisees saw this, they said to his disciples, "Why does your teacher eat with tax collectors and sinners?"

—Matthew 9:10–11

FOR MANY, THE IDEA OF A DINNER PARTY HAS MORE negative than positive associations. Leaving aside the challenges of the menu, food shopping, and cooking, the main problem is often the guest list. Who should be invited—or not? Sometimes dinner parties (even among family) are matters of obligation rather than celebration. Certain birthday parties are nonnegotiable. Thanksgiving or Christmas dinners *must* alternate between one side of a couple's family and the other. Then there are the anxieties associated with *being* invited or not. How many of us have been deeply wounded by *not* being included? Not chosen for the team. Not selected for membership in the club. Overlooked or bypassed or avoided.

Dinner parties can be reminders of all the pain that goes with interpersonal relationships—and they can be the greatest occasions of joy and life-giving connection, meals that heal old wounds and restore broken relationships and give birth to new communities. A most remarkable film features this theme. *Babette's Feast*, the 1987 film based on a story by Isak Dinesen, is about an exiled Parisian chef who seeks refuge with two elderly sisters who lead a small community of Lutheran pietists on the coast of Denmark. A once-vibrant community has dwindled over time. The aging members relive old grudges. When a letter arrives saying that Babette has won the lottery, she decides to spend her entire winnings on preparing a true feast for the otherwise abstemious elders. The day comes, and although they pledge not to "enjoy" these worldly pleasures, the wine flows and so does conversation, and a few confessions, and, ultimately, healing. This joyful feast rekindles faith and rebuilds community and brings life anew.

There are many, many stories in the Gospels that feature Jesus at table with others—friends and enemies; the curious, the critical, the devoted. The parables of Jesus also feature dinner parties and wedding banquets. By the time the Gospels were written, Christian worship included sharing bread and wine. Thus, the Gospel stories are shaped by Christian practice, even as the practice itself is informed by stories from the Jesus tradition.

These stories about sharing meals have embedded in them at least three symbolic themes. First, a great banquet (particularly, a wedding feast) has been a symbol for the future that God has promised Israel since the time of Isaiah, so when Jesus compares the kingdom of God to someone who hosts a banquet, he is recalling Isaiah's vision of a meal that not only welcomes all but also signals the end of death (see Isa. 25:6–7). Second, meals always involve extending and receiving hospitality. But for all the examples of human hospitality, what stands behind all of this is God's hospitality to us: "You prepare a table before me in the presence of my enemies . . . my cup overflows" (Ps. 23:5). Third, eating with others is an ethical or moral matter. In the ancient world, it was understood that sharing a meal created or cemented a relationship. Thus, it mattered with whom you "broke bread," which is what makes Jesus' practice of eating with whoever invited him all the more noteworthy.

Which brings us to the story of Jesus and Matthew (or as Mark and Luke call him, "Levi"). Jesus is strolling through Capernaum and passes by the booth where Matthew is doing his job collecting taxes. Probably to the amazement of all (including Matthew), Jesus says to him, "Follow me," and he does. In the next scene, Matthew hosts a big dinner party for Jesus and his other disciples . . . and the rest of Matthew's friends. Since Matthew's work made him deeply suspect by nearly everybody, his friends were people like himself: tax collectors and sinners.

Of all the criticisms of Jesus, this (along

with healing on the Sabbath) is the most frequent: "He eats with tax collectors and sinners" (see Luke 15:1–2 and the story of Zacchaeus, Luke 19:1–10). What exactly was the problem with tax collectors? Scholars today tell us that collecting taxes in the Roman Empire was a franchise business operation. Collecting taxes for the region of Judea or Galilee, for example, would be put out to bid. The one who won the bid hired others who lived in various villages or towns to collect the tax revenue from their neighbors. Rome specified how much it expected in net revenue, but it was understood that the various tax collectors along the way could "gross up" the taxes as their fees. Obviously, this system was ripe for exploitation, but it was exacerbated by the fact that the tax ultimately was going to Rome. Thus, tax collectors were widely seen as traitors to their own people. (The term "sinners" is a little more difficult to define. At the least, these were folk whom the "good people" thought of as disreputable.)

Understanding the contempt that both religious leaders and ordinary people had for people like Matthew is critical to understanding this story and the dinner party. The "call of Matthew" is first of all just that: a "call story." It mirrors the calling of Simon and Andrew, James and John. In fact, Matthew is the only other one of the twelve whose call story is recorded. Just like the first four, Matthew gets up immediately and follows Jesus. I've always imagined that these calls didn't exactly come out of the blue. I suspect that all these folk knew Jesus—had heard him teach and watched him reach out to those in pain. Jesus was a magnet for those who were ready for a new life. The Synoptic Gospels describe "the twelve" as an inner circle of sorts. Legends developed around their later exploits, but here it is worth noting that fully one-fourth of Jesus' choices were curious at best: in addition to Matthew, the traitor-cheat-tax collector, there are Simon the Zealot (meaning he was, or had been, a firebrand, revolutionary) and Judas Iscariot, the betrayer.

Second, this call story is also a story of healing. The clue is in the way Jesus responds to his critics: "Those who are well have no need of a physician, but those who are sick [do]" (Matt. 9:13). This story in which the tax collector walks away from his former life to follow Jesus is placed in between two collections of healing stories (Matt. 8:28–9:8 and 9:18–34). In the ancient world, one of the few treatments for illness was isolation or quarantine. Thus, when someone was restored to health, they were able to return to their friends and families. This is precisely what Jesus does here: he ends the ostracism that Matthew and friends experienced. He restores them to community by including them in his fellowship. Luke makes the same point when he uses the criticism of eating with tax collectors as the prompt for three parables about something which is lost being found and someone being restored to the family where he belongs (cf. Luke 15).

Finally, this is a story about mercy. Jesus quotes Hosea 6:6 when he says, "I desire mercy, not sacrifice." Offering sacrifices to God had been a cornerstone of Jewish worship for at least a thousand years. Periodically in life (after the birth of a child, for example) and at the time of major festivals, people brought an offering of an animal or bird or the "first fruits" of the harvest to present to God as expressions of gratitude. Sacrifices accompanied prayers of petition. They could also be signs of repentance or requests for forgiveness. Sacrifice was prayer enacted. And that is not *unimportant*, Jesus says. It's just that these significant rituals are secondary to acts of mercy or compassion. God's mercy is everlasting. Jesus is the mercy of God in human form, never more so than when he eats with outcasts and welcomes all of us in our brokenness.

Who belongs and who doesn't? Who is welcomed and who is held at arm's length? How wide are the boundaries of our community? Our worshiping community? Our nation? Churches have struggled with these questions since the beginning. Was the good news only for Jews or was it also for Gentiles? And if so, on what terms? Those questions are debated and answered in Acts and in Paul's letters to the Galatians and Romans in particular. White American Christians asked those questions about the Africans they enslaved. Various denominations have asked about the place of LGBTQ members in Christian fellowship and some churches have divided because of it. But we know the answer given in the New Testament: welcome wins. Inclusion wins. The wideness of God's mercy reaches out to those on whatever margins society creates.

Hospitality transforms all who are involved. Host and guest are impacted and changed by the relationships that are formed in the breaking and sharing of bread. This is precisely why integrating lunch counters during the civil rights struggle was such a powerful symbol: because everyone knew, deep down, that if white and Black people ate together as equals, as fellow citizens, as sisters and brothers in the family of God, the walls of segregation would collapse. And they did. Both as churches and as a nation, we still have a long way to go before we have tables where all are welcome. But all of us who have experienced the power of breaking bread with those from whom we have been separated or estranged know that we come away not only changed, but free.

ARTIST'S REFLECTION

Our text is the story of Jesus meeting a tax collector to whom he extends the invitation to "follow." It is a story of calling, invitation, and inclusion. Apparently, Matthew accepts, and the next scene shows Jesus and the tax collector sitting down to dinner. Not surprisingly, as this event is observed by others, questions arise:

"Why?" Why would the teacher, Jesus, gather with the selfish, untrustworthy outcast who collaborates with the Romans and cheats his fellow Judeans—and even eat with him? For Jesus, the issue is clear, and when he speaks in Matthew 9:12–13, he attempts to clarify the issue for his religious critics: "Those who are well have no need of a physician, but those who are sick. Go and learn what this means, 'I desire mercy, not sacrifice.' For I have come to call not the righteous but sinners." In other words, living is not about appearances, rituals, reputations, or expectations. It is about sincerity, mercy, healing, and love. This perspective does not dismiss the Jewish sacrificial system but clarifies the spiritual logic behind it. These are the values so prominent in Jesus' ministry.

As I imagined this scenario playing out in a modern context, I thought about the economic and cultural diversity that exists in our individual lives. We may respect the viewpoints of others. We may feel compassion for those who are less fortunate. And we may seek ways to make the world a better place for all people. These are noble gestures. But the real challenge of this story may be one of inclusion. Inclusion is much more difficult than tolerating and respecting from a distance. Inclusion challenges us to engage, to sit down together, to be in the moment with those whom we don't know well enough to trust.

Progressive Christians often think of Jesus as catering exclusively to the disenfranchised and the poor. But the reality is that the Gospels present a Jesus who gives equal time to the scholars and the wealthy. The Jesus of the Gospels did not spend his time with just one demographic group. He dined with sinners and tax collectors, and also with respected Pharisees and elites. So, I imagined a table with extremes. How often, if ever, have we observed a setting where a man dressed in a suit, with the trappings of money and success, is sitting adjacent to a man in the dirty, worn clothing expressive of homelessness or poverty? Such an image invites us to imagine the conversation that would emerge.

Perhaps the man in the suit is an accomplished banker or investor who has served his community and been both a philanthropist and ideal citizen. Perhaps he represents what we all want to be.

Or perhaps, he is a selfish scoundrel who has attained his wealth by mistreating the poor and taking advantage of the less fortunate.

Perhaps the poorly dressed man is lazy, unemployed, and unsupportive of his family. Or he could be a hardworking man down on his luck, transitioning into a new life that will be rewarding in new ways, a man that looks out for those around him in ways that only he can.

Most of us acknowledge that one cannot know these realities by trusting our snap judgments from visual cues. But we also must acknowledge that we bring preconceived values and attitudes to every experience we have, which shape our interpretations. And the critical question for us is: how do these perceptions shape our behavior?

QUESTIONS FOR REFLECTION

1. Are dinner parties and holiday gatherings more a cause of stress or excitement for you? Is it the interpersonal aspect or the planning and preparation that are more challenging for you?

2. What does it mean to you that imagery of a great banquet in Scripture often symbolizes the culmination of God's work in the world, the end of death, a day when all people are gathered together in true relationship with one another?

3. What groups of people today tend to be viewed the way "tax collectors and sinners" were in Jesus' day? Have you ever been shamed for who you eat with or keep company with?

4. How might we help "heal" the suffering and ostracism that such people experience? Does the author's comparison with integrated lunch

counters during the civil rights movement give you any ideas? (See p. 25.)

5. Are there times when you choose "sacrifice" over "mercy" when it comes to practicing the radical hospitality Jesus models for us and to which God calls us?

6. Consider this chapter's illustration of a rich and poor man sitting side by side. Imagine you are observing this scene at the counter of a diner. What assumptions might you have about the two men? What might happen as you watch them interact?

Chapter 3

SURPRISED BY GRACE

Dinner Interrupted

READ: LUKE 7:36–50

And a woman in the city, who was a sinner, having learned that he was eating in the Pharisee's house, brought an alabaster jar of ointment. She stood behind him at his feet, weeping, and began to bathe his feet with her tears and to dry them with her hair.

—Luke 7:37–38a

SEVERAL YEARS AGO, THE TV SHOW *SATURDAY NIGHT Live* sought to tackle the awkwardness of Thanksgiving dinner. In the segment, a family is gathered around a table. Three generations are present: sweet grandparents, their bickering daughters with their spouses, and a grandchild. The dinner begins with niceties and quiet, if stilted, conversation. But quickly, the conversation shifts as one of the daughters begins sharing her political opinions. The other daughter, obviously in disagreement, rolls her eyes and shoots her a disapproving glare. Unphased, the woman continues her political diatribe and, in response, her sister slams down her fork as if ready for a fight. But just as things seem like they might come to blows, the granddaughter runs to a stereo and hits play. And out of the stereo comes the song "Hello" from the acclaimed singer Adele. Suddenly the conflict at the table pauses as each person seems transported, lip-syncing the infectious song. But then, with the music finished, the bickering returns—one time over politics, one time over sports, other times over long-held family disputes. But each time the conflict gets too heated, the granddaughter runs for the stereo. The skit goes back and forth, showing again and again how family conflict gets interrupted by the distracting melody, until eventually everyone is transported from their Thanksgiving table into a kind of unified euphoria, all centering around the interruption of Adele's amazing voice. It is a great example of how a welcomed interruption can smooth over the toughest family dinner.

Here we get the story of just such an interrupted table. A dinner party that certainly didn't go the way that anyone expected it to. Our story comes from Luke's Gospel at just the point in Jesus' ministry when he was beginning to get a reputation. He had performed healings and exorcisms. Crowds were following him wherever he went, so buzz was building about this rabbi who taught about the kingdom of God. Simon, who was a Pharisee, must have thought it quite amusing to think of hosting this Jesus for dinner with his friends. It's no wonder, then, that Jesus was received with less than stellar hospitality. He was less a guest of honor and more the evening's entertainment. But while it seems they expected the wild antics of his cousin, John the Baptist, this Jesus turned out to be cool and knowledgeable, interesting and engaging. He himself was not the oddity that night. Rather, it was the crowd that followed him that caused a stir.

We can almost picture the crowd sitting outside of Simon's home, peering through the windows, not wanting to miss the chance to see Jesus do something extraordinary. While

Jesus' presence did not initially seem to make that dinner party particularly eventful, the presence of another did. We're told she was a sinner and nothing more. History often paints her as a prostitute, but nothing in any of the Gospels indicates that. She was simply a sinner, like all of us, and it seems everyone at Simon's party knew it. Despite the crowd waiting for Jesus beyond the walls, this woman felt she could not wait. She had to meet and honor Jesus. So, she came into Simon's home with her alabaster jar full of oil, scandalizing everyone there just by her presence. She knelt behind Jesus, and as she did, her eyes filled with tears. Tears upon tears upon tears. So many, in fact, that she washed his feet with them. And not having a cloth, she had to make do with what she had. She took down her hair—another scandal—unknotted it and wiped her tears from his feet. And then she anointed his feet with precious, costly oil that must have cost her everything she had.

This is an intimate scene—a scene that may make us uncomfortable, just as it did those dinner guests. In that age, the heads of priests, kings, or prophets may have been publicly anointed. The body was anointed as an act of hospitality or preparation for burial. But the public anointing of the feet *only* was an unheard-of act in antiquity. A man may have had his wife or daughter or slave anoint his feet in private, but in public, this was not only strange but shocking.

So much so that here we are, two thousand years later, still discussing it: this act of devotion that interrupted the well-laid plans of that evening.

Now, there are many layers of interruption that can be found in this story. First, there is the interruption of the dinner party itself, and Simon's pointed examination of Jesus. For these guests who were excited to see who this new radical was, their curiosity was interrupted. But so, too, was Jesus. This woman also intruded on Jesus' efforts to "play it cool." Jesus, who was criticized for being "a friend of tax collectors and sinners," was just as able to engage with the religious elites—as he was with the poor. Here he was a dinner guest at the Pharisees' party, and her intrusive, tearful act of devotion must have made that entire room uncomfortable. She interrupted his best efforts at passing—at engaging these guests who were watching him and making assumptions. Her intimate act interrupted all of that, making them recoil and think him even more radical.

But that night, while dinner plans and social norms were interrupted, so too was a simple, if not usually public, act of devotion. Her plans were interrupted too. The woman, we read, having learned that Jesus was eating at Simon's house, brought an alabaster jar of ointment to anoint his feet. But we read that something—and we don't know what—brought her to tears that night. So many tears, in fact, that she could wash his feet in them.

When I read this story of this woman's tears, it reminds of another story. It's a story about a kid named Billy, a good kid who just always found himself in the wrong place at the wrong time. He would ride his bike to his friends' house each day over the summer. And like a gang of ten-year-olds does, they would own their town. They would play in ditches and ride their bikes through drive-throughs. They would explore country roads and set elaborate pranks. But one day this crew got a bit too mischievous. On a dare, Billy ran into a neighbor's yard and stole vegetables from her garden. He jumped on his bike and made his getaway; he was now legendary in the group. But that afternoon, when he came home and laid his bike against the house wall, his guilt was overwhelming him. He knew his mother was going to ask how his day was and he knew he was going to have to lie. When he walked in the house, there she was. Her face lit up with love as she asked him how his day was, and despite all his best-laid plans to tell a tale, he took one look at his mother and burst into tears. He cried and he cried and he cried. And she just held him. Of course, she knew what he'd done—it was a small town and the neighbor lady had called. But she didn't get into it with him—she just held him and let him cry, let him know how much she loved him.

I wonder if that woman, at Simon's dinner party, had a similar reaction. I wonder if, perhaps, tears were not included in her plan for that evening. She came with her alabaster jar of ointment, but maybe she simply planned to anoint his feet in an effort to shock these religious leaders. A kind of civil disobedience against these haughty, judgmental elites. Whatever her intention for that night, something about seeing Jesus interrupted her plans, and like a guilt-ridden child upon seeing a loving parent, she just cried. And cried. And cried. No words needed. Something in the comfort of his presence made her know she was forgiven—whatever her sin. And what better response to such grace than tears?

Interruptions, we all know, can be frustrating. Many of us are planners who map out every detail according to the vision in our heads. We plan outings and dinner parties and Thanksgiving meals far in advance in the hopes of managing whatever crisis or issue may arise. But sometimes, despite it all, interruptions stop us in our tracks. Sometimes, as in that *Saturday Night Live* skit, they bring us together. They stop our bickering and our fighting; they help us come together around some common good. But sometimes interruptions can also have the opposite effect. Like for Simon, who simply drew inward, whispering to himself and his friends how displeased he was, how uncomfortable he was with what was transpiring.

Christ, it seems, used interruptions as teachable moments. A time for parables. A time for vision. A time for pausing and considering: what can be learned here? This woman came and, seeing Christ, burst into tears. Tears of guilt? Maybe. But also tears of joy and of healing and of transformation. Tears shed when one's life was interrupted by grace.

Maybe we need to ask ourselves how we respond to such interruptions? To such grace?

As we continue our journey through the season of Lent, may we be open to the interruptions that might meet us along the way. May we take them as opportunities for growth and learning. May we shake off the Simon inside us, who would rather mumble disapprovingly. And instead, may we take those interruptions for what they are: opportunities. Opportunities for growth, opportunities for love, opportunities for grace. Grace so overwhelming it needs no words. Grace so amazing it brings us to tears.

ARTIST'S REFLECTION

Interruption. Surprise. Shock. An experience common to human existence. The room described is filled with men reclining at table with their heads near the table of food. This was the Greco-Roman practice of eating. While the men talk, the woman enters and takes her place behind Jesus without speaking a word. She need not say anything. It is her actions that are shocking and in stark contrast to the others already in the room. She weeps, and she lets her tears fall on Jesus, which she then wipes with her hair. It is a very intimate scene. Why is she doing this? There is a reference to forgiveness, but the discussion reveals that the motivation is love, and the text seems to emphasize that we are not witnessing forgiveness that is a result of love, but love that is a result of forgiveness. This is born out in the conversation between Jesus and Simon. Simon acknowledges Jesus as teacher and Jesus teaches Simon by way of a story and question, suggesting that those who experience great forgiveness will naturally show great love. We are not told any details of the forgiveness the unnamed woman has experienced, just that she is a sinner, obviously in need of forgiveness. The others in the room see her as utterly "other," but we know that is not Jesus' perspective.

The challenge to us in the modern world is clear. The need to be forgiven and the need to forgive is essential to community. In the ancient context, "sinner" is an exclusionary term that describes someone undeserving of, or removed from, community. We may not use the word in the same way today, but we exclude others for many reasons. Sometimes we think of our own values or morality as superior to others, but this text challenges us to rethink our assumption. We are challenged by this story to recognize how fragile our community can be. Apparent differences in political and theological views can lead to people being pushed to the periphery of their community, with little hope of restored relationships. Too often we redefine our truth to support our exclusionary behavior. We all need forgiveness and restoration. And we all need to participate in the process of forgiving others.

All of this is profoundly implied when the woman who doesn't belong walks into the room. I chose to illustrate this biblical setting because it is likely to be an unusual scene for the modern reader. When the style of seating is visually presented, the reality of how a woman might enter and move behind the men to one's lounging feet emphasizes the potential shock—shock that could happen to every one of us in our own modern experiences in different ways. Thus, the illustration is about capturing that moment of truth when the woman enters and bravely speaks her truth with vulnerable actions. It invites us to consider whose presence in our homes or lives might unsettle, startle, or alarm us.

QUESTIONS FOR REFLECTION

1. How do you feel about being interrupted while speaking or in the middle of a task or meal? What distinguishes a good interruption from a bad one?

2. Why was the behavior of this woman with the alabaster jar so scandalous? What would be a comparably scandalous interruption today?

3. The author notes how different characters in the story experienced interruption in different ways (see pp. 37–38). Which of these interruptions is most intriguing or compelling to you? Why?

4. Why do you think the woman was moved to tears? What do you think of the author's suggestion that her actions were intended as a type of protest against Simon and the other Pharisees, "a kind of civil disobedience against these haughty, judgmental elites" (pp. 39–40)?

5. How can interruptions be an opportunity? How might you prepare yourself to look for the opportunity in the next interruption you experience?

6. The illustration for this chapter does not offer many clues as to which figure might be Jesus. Who do you think Jesus might be in this scene, and why do you draw that conclusion?

Chapter 4

RELATIONSHIPS AND RECIPROCITY

Making Room at the Table

READ: LUKE 14:7–14

"But when you are invited, go and sit down at the lowest place, so that when your host comes, he may say to you, 'Friend, move up higher'; then you will be honored in the presence of all who sit at the table with you. For all who exalt themselves will be humbled, and those who humble themselves will be exalted."

—Luke 14:10–11

JESUS' PARABLE OF SEATING ARRANGEMENTS BRINGS to mind memories of meals shared around our family dining table: who sat where, and how the seating arrangements shifted as family came to town. Who made space, I find myself wondering, when my grandparents visited and my Poppy claimed the table's head? Who moved to make that shift possible? And just how many leaves did that simple dining table have that as the guest list grew, room was always made? There was always enough.

Recent shifts in home design indicate a trend in homes being built without a dining room altogether. This change accommodates the needs of families for space and allows a kind of hospitality made real in the everyday, rather than just the occasional. Nonetheless, the sense of place can still be understood. One longs for the place of honor. The place closest to the host or the most interesting guest. The spot right by that grandparent who can make you laugh or that aunt whom you have always adored. There is something about one's place while eating that carries importance. Where you sit means something.

Of course, in Jesus' day, dining arrangements would have looked different than what we now imagine. Male guests would have been reclining on couches, rather than sitting in chairs, and those sitting on the center couch—the place of honor—would have been the guests who held the greatest wealth, power, or office. It would not have been uncommon for the seating to constantly be changing as more prestigious men came in, requiring the lower-ranking guests to move down to a location farther from the place of honor.

Into that setting, Jesus decides to share a parable. Perhaps he is recalling Proverbs 25:6–7: "Do not put yourself forward in the king's presence or stand in the place of the great; for it is better to be told, 'Come up here,' than to be put lower in the presence of a noble." Similarly, Jesus says that one should not choose the seat of honor when they arrive at a party, "for all who exalt themselves will be humbled, and those who humble themselves will be exalted."

But then he takes the parable a step farther.

"When you give a luncheon or a dinner," Jesus says, "do not invite your friends or your brothers or your relatives or rich neighbors. . . . But . . . invite the poor, the crippled, the lame, and the blind. And you will be blessed, because they cannot repay you" (Luke 14:12b–14a).

Now, obviously, this characterization of those with impairments—whether social or physical—sounds condescending to our modern ears. To imply that one's differing ability might impair them from participating in society feels belittling. And yet, during Jesus' day—and for the context of the dinner party—it was true, because special events required a give and take; an "I'll scratch your back if you'll scratch mine" kind of relationship. And those pushed to the edge of society, those marginalized by physical condition or lack of wealth, simply could not participate.

Jesus' parable of the dinner party (which, quite frankly, feels very "on the nose" for these men who are, in fact, sitting at a dinner party) raises the dangers of *transactional relationships*. In particular, transactional relationships that obscure our best efforts at real hospitality. Transactional relationships are those relationships based in quid pro quo, a phrase from Latin that literally means "something for something." I invite you to a party, for example, and expect that you will invite me back. Or I connect you with a job opening, and expect that when my time comes, you will help me accordingly.

It's the sentiment behind comments we still use frequently—"I owe you a lunch!" or "We really need to have them over for dinner." There's something obligatory about the relationships.

Some inherent mutual understanding of give and receive. But when Jesus sits at table in this passage—when he looks around this room of Pharisees who have invited him, yet again, to dinner, Jesus says to them—through a parable—"we are capable of so much more than this."

Jesus is inviting them to move from *transactional relationships* to *transformational relationships*. To move from survival-based, get-what-I-need kinds of relationships, to table-turning, "reign of God" kinds of relationships. Relationships where traditional tables are flipped, and doors are opened, and the leaves come out, and bread is broken—together—with all of God's children. Be mindful of who has a seat at the table, we hear Jesus teaching. It's not just a lesson about where people are seated. No, it is about *who* has a place; who is invited. And the power of this parable goes far beyond the dining room. Far beyond the home, even. It is a lesson that can apply to work, to school, to sports teams, to book clubs. It is a lesson that even applies to the church.

You know, it wasn't so long ago that the kind of transactional relationships Jesus is talking about were on full display front and center in houses of worship. Following the Protestant Reformation, worshipers who traditionally would have stood or kneeled or sat on the floor in worship, suddenly began building pews to accommodate lengthy sermons and worship services with little room for interaction. Consequently, the wealthiest families in the congregation would pay to have the best pews—pews that were often custom built by each congregation's wealthiest families, who held actual deeds to them and passed them down to their children. Like a huge dinner party set around the table, the seating arrangements communicated who had the power, with the wealthiest owning their pews near the front and the poorest being relegated to the back or the balcony. And even as people railed more and more against this system, it took centuries to undo it because it was a transactional kind of relationship. It took money to build and maintain a church. And those people who paid for their pews made the church's finances possible. They kept the church open. So, what's a little hierarchical seating arrangement in the grand scheme of things?

Well, according to our parable for today, it's everything. According to Jesus, the privilege that allows some to have a place over others, the privilege that allows some to have influence and power at the expense of others—that is a relationship driven by fear, driven by the give-and-take system we have created for worldly survival—a give-and-take system that is far from the kingdom Jesus envisions.

Of course, this system is not isolated to church pews or dining room tables. It is not unique to the upper echelon or to those wielding the greatest power. No, that give-and-take system can still play out in our church meetings (who has attended longest?) and our board meetings (who has the most connections?). And it can even still be seen around our churches, where rooms bear the names of the greatest donors. But in the kingdom of God, Jesus tells us that we are invited to more. We are invited to root our relationships in faith and love and, more than anything, in trust—trust in the God who can open our doors and expand our tables, who can free us from worrying about how we will be compensated or what will be offered in return.

Christ's table invites us to pay attention to who has a place—in our church, in our community, in our world. Who has a place at the table and what is driving that seating arrangement? Is it power? Is it influence? Is it privilege? Or is it trust? World-changing, love-lifting, transformational trust. Christ's words invite us to trust that our survival is not dependent on repaying favors or restricting the seating arrangement. Instead, Christ invites us to trust in the God who opens our doors, who makes room at our tables, and always provides enough. Jesus proclaimed a God whose bread will never run out, whose hospitality is endless, and whose grace can overturn the tables of our weary world. Christ invites us to trust and to set our tables accordingly. Our dining room tables, our board room tables, our classroom tables. Christ invites us to make our world more like God's world, where there is always enough and all God's people have a place.

ARTIST'S REFLECTION

Imagine walking into a formal banquet hall fit for royalty and being the first to arrive and the first to choose a seat. One would think carefully about where to sit. This challenge is the setting of this text in which Jesus provides practical advice to be careful where you first choose to sit. Clearly, he has observed some who think highly of themselves and are quick to choose the more important seats. The banquet setting is both the description of the place where the story is happening, a Sabbath meal, and simultaneously a metaphor for the kingdom of God or a community of early Christians. Perhaps it was intended to represent the early community of believers who gathered at the time of the writer of this Gospel.

The issue of importance and priority is the issue underlying the story. We spend so much of our time trying to justify our importance in the world. We want to be influencers; we long to have a defined legacy that matters. If anyone suggests otherwise, our sensibilities are insulted. Can there be both this sense of self-worth and real humility? It seems like that should be possible, as Jesus seems to suggest. Perhaps understanding this paradox requires a more complete understanding of the values that Jesus promoted. The stories of Jesus at table throughout the Bible consistently reinforce the notion that Jesus is about the business of "feeding people." This is both a physical and spiritual notion. It is the hunger of the people and Jesus' love for such people that makes them worthy—not status or accomplishment.

As we imagine ourselves in the glamorous banquet hall of the illustration, we are challenged to see ourselves on a spectrum of worthiness. In this piece, I imagined entering a room that reeked of old money and well-developed expectations, casting doubts on my own status. The pressure to determine one's standing becomes greater when one is the first to arrive. This image should conjure up discomfort in nearly every observer. There will always be those with higher status than we have (based on worldly standards). And there will always be those whom the world sees as below our level. We must focus on where God sees us. I believe that in God's mind we are all of value. When we encounter the Jesus of the Bible, he tends to be less concerned about behavior modification and more concerned about meeting needs and helping people know how much they are loved by God.

QUESTIONS FOR REFLECTION

1. Are the seating arrangements in your house based on status/seniority, practicality, or some other reasoning? What happens when someone sits in a place that is someone else's usual seat?

2. How often do you let quid pro quo or reciprocity guide your actions when considering whom to invite to a gathering or how much to spend on a gift? What do you think Jesus would say about this way of thinking?

3. Churches no longer let people purchase pews to reserve their spot and display their status. In what ways might the church still enable quid pro quo thinking among its members, and how

might it practice Jesus' admonition to invite and welcome those who cannot repay?

4. Given that Jesus is giving this pointed instruction about dinner party behavior *at* a dinner party, how do you think people may have responded?

5. How do you need to trust God when it comes to your status or positioning in society?

6. For the illustrator, a grand banquet hall stirs up status anxiety. In what context do you become most anxious about your value and place?

Chapter 5

EXCUSES AND INVITATIONS

Empty Chairs at the Table

READ: LUKE 14:15–24

"Then the owner of the house became angry and said to his slave, 'Go out at once into the streets and lanes of the town and bring in the poor, the crippled, the blind, and the lame.' And the slave said, 'Sir, what you ordered has been done, and there is still room.' Then the master said to the slave, 'Go out into the roads and lanes, and compel people to come in, so that my house may be filled.'"

—Luke 14:21b–23

HAVE YOU EVER HAD TO MAKE AN EXCUSE FOR MISSing a big event? Maybe it was honest—some real conflict that you could do nothing about. Maybe it was less so—some paltry tale concocted to make both you and your host believe that you were unable to come. Today's time at table with Jesus invites us to consider what happens when we make excuses—how God reacts; what, in turn, God does.

I'll never forget, back in 2020, the conversation I had with my parents over the phone. It was the week before Thanksgiving and COVID was raging. Vaccines seemed far beyond anyone's reach at that point. Life was still mostly on lockdown. I had to make one of the most difficult phone calls I've ever made to say that we couldn't come to Thanksgiving. It was a legitimate excuse—nothing made up, no underlying desire to get out of *that* party. But it was painful, all around. You can ask my parents what their response was—sadness, anger? But that was just one of many such phone calls made in the course of 2020. I think many of us took comfort in knowing we weren't alone in making that decision. That same phone call was being made the country over, leaving empty spots at what were usually full family dinner tables.

There were so many of those empty spots that year. And, sadly, there will be many more, after more than 6 million people worldwide have died from COVID-19. More than one million alone in the United States. And that is only from COVID-19. It doesn't account for the empty chairs left by cancer. Or the empty chairs left by heart disease. Or the empty chairs left by time's relentless march forward. Looking at those tables, those spots left empty, can leave a host filled with sadness. With grief. With anger.

When Jesus tells his story of a dinner banquet, it is hard to say how legitimate the excuses are that the host is given. One person has bought land and must see it; another has five yoke of oxen that must be tried out; and still another begs off for marital reasons. Some read these excuses as legitimate reasons for missing the banquet—reasons tied to one's economic and social obligations. Others read them as an effort at wriggling out of attendance. But regardless of the legitimacy of the excuse made, one thing is clear. Imagining those tables left empty makes the host angry. Angry that his generosity has been treated so flippantly. Angry that their absence could cause his own embarrassment. Angry that he now must save face and find substitutes to fill their now empty places around his banquet table.

Now remember: Jesus is telling this story to a group of Pharisees who, themselves, are gathered at table together. Who, themselves, are part of that social elite that this host was seeking out for his party. Up until this point, they "get" exactly what the host in this story is going through—they get the etiquette of party invites and RSVP's; they get the presumed guest list and who should be at table at such a banquet; and maybe they, too, get the frustration at excuses, which robs one's banquet of its people. They get it: empty chairs and tables are frustrating.

But then Jesus takes it a step further.

In the story, the host tells his slave, "Go out at once into the streets and lanes of the town and bring in the poor, the crippled, the blind, and the lame." Forget the social order, the host says, and fill up this table. Forget replacing people of status with people of status. Forget it all and fill this table up. Raymond Prickett writes, "[T]he parable . . . features an elite person for whom the ethic of reciprocity has worked well until . . . he is rebuffed by his peers. His response is one of anger, and that anger motivates him to break with the social order."[1]

"Go out" the host says, "and bring in the poor, the crippled, the blind, and the lame." The exact same list Jesus mentions just a few verses before, to this same group of Pharisees, gathered at this same meal. Tables and chairs filled, not by the who's who of this world, but by the who's who of the kingdom of God. Which leaves those Pharisees, and us the reader, to wonder: what excuse would we make to avoid a seat at such a banquet?

A real-life parable is told of a man named Martin Rinkart, a humble Lutheran parish priest who served in Germany during Europe's Thirty Years' War. Germany at that time had been devastated by famine, disease, and destruction from war, and then to top it all off, the plague came. Rinkart was said to have performed funerals for 40 to 50 people per day—a total of over 4,000. In that time, history tells us, he buried his children and his wife. This man, who could

1. Raymond Pickett, "Luke 14:15–24, Exegetical Perspective" *Feasting on the Gospels: Luke, Volume 2* (Louisville, KY: Westminster John Knox Press, 2014), 71.

easily have looked at the tragedy around him—at the tables left empty and the chairs whose seats would go unfilled—and given up, lost faith, and lost hope. No one could have blamed him for that. But instead, he wrote a song—a song to sing at the table, before the meal, to help him remain focused on the blessings he still had. The beloved hymn, "Now Thank We All Our God" (*Glory to God,* 643), was written by a man who could have looked with despair at the tables left empty in his home and throughout his community, and instead persevered, day by day, meal by meal, through a practice of gratitude. This gratitude saved not only him, but the hearts of so many shaken by devastating loss.

Our Scripture focus for this chapter invites the question of how we respond in the face of the chairs and tables left empty—left empty by flippant excuses, left empty by severed relationships, left empty by death. How does our grief and sadness, our anger and mourning transform us? How does it reshape us, those empty expected responses that may try to fill those spaces left empty in our lives; that may try to put a Band-Aid over our wounded pride, or broken hearts? How can the table transform us toward something more, something expansive, something unexpected?

More than anything, though, this passage for today is all about the realm of God—the great banquet of eternity to which we all have an invitation. It picks up on themes found throughout Scripture, story after story telling of God's lavish generosity, liberality, and extravagance. Of weddings and banquets, dedications, and offerings. And in Christ, of God showing that extravagant goodness and mercy like no other. Tangibly, walking through landscapes, teaching on hillsides, sitting at table, and breaking bread to show—to demonstrate—the breadth of God's love, the extravagance of God's welcome.

This extravagance is offered even in the face of excuses, even in the face of sadness and disappointment, frustration, and yes, even anger. Extravagance that is offered even in the face of tables not yet filled and chairs that are empty. An extravagant love that never quits. It just keeps expanding. Growing larger, pushing outward, drawing in the ones from the fringes and finding them a place at the table. Going into the roads and lanes, the hillsides and seashores and inviting people to come, to find a seat, to be part of the great banquet that has no end, that will never be filled, that will always have enough. It is a feast of plenty, where there is always room. And where Christ, our host, would have us sit.

In this season of Lent, this passage invites us to imagine Christ's table and to find ourselves there. To find ourselves among those who are grieving and mourning, among those who have suffered unspeakable loss or have been abandoned by their dearest loves; among those who are angry at justice left undone and who feel pushed to the fringes by an unfair social order; to find ourselves among the who's who of God's kingdom, knowing we always have a place if only we will accept the invitation.

So may it be that we will not hesitate or search for excuses when it comes to the kingdom of God. May it be that we will not give into that urge to give up in the face of our own sadness and grief, anger and longing, but that as God's own, we might allow such feelings to open our hearts to all God's people longing for a home and a welcome. And may it be that at that table we might find ourselves transformed by the love and extravagant generosity of Christ, our King, who will always make room, who will always prepare a seat, and who will always have bread enough to break for all God's people.

As it is at Christ's table, may it be so at our own.

ARTIST'S REFLECTION

The story that follows the challenge of where to sit at the banquet doesn't conclude the challenges of Jesus' teaching at this particular dinner party. Questions of who should be invited and who should be left out abound in this parable. The reader is forced to consider what makes real and authentic community. Certainly, there is an expectation of inviting the typical neighbors, those who are likely to return the favor. However, when they refuse, an alternative guest list must be considered. The meal should not be wasted; community is still needed. So, the host invites those who would not have originally come to mind but who appear to be available. Perhaps there is a harsh lesson here for the initial invitees, but the bigger question is: What is the commentary on community created by the initial excuses? The host doesn't seem to think positively about the responses of the initial invitees; rather, he seems frustrated. I believe this is an attempt by the storyteller to ensure that the listeners and readers recognize the lack of honest and sincere interest in the relationship being expressed. Community cannot succeed without commitment, care, and honesty. For community to be effective, everyone must be comfortable being their authentic selves and not obsessed with false representation to keep up appearances. And there must be commitment to unselfish behavior that enriches the whole community.

If we see ourselves as the original invitees

in this story, we are challenged to think about the excuses and misrepresentations we often produce when we are invited to share our honest perspectives. Our churches are full of pretenders who feel that if they express their true selves or expose their vulnerability, bad things can happen.

This thinking inspired my approach to the illustration. I imagined a traditional potluck dinner hosted by nearly every church that has ever existed in modern America. Who is invited? With whom do we sit? Do we make extra effort to make everyone feel welcome? How do we encourage authentic sharing, authentic diversity, and authentic acceptance? We may avoid the real truth in lieu of community-sanctioned truth that only reinforces our own membership.

What if our church communities invested their time in reaching out to those who are not obviously part of the dominant culture? What if churches made a priority of seeking out those who have disappeared as much as we emphasize the need to connect to the big financial contributors? We spend our time polishing our worship, stocking our coffee bars, and making sure we entertain. What if we understood our primary obligation as a church was to set the table for nonjudgmental community?

QUESTIONS FOR REFLECTION

1. Have you ever made up an excuse to decline an invitation? Do you think the excuses of the original invitees in this parable were legitimate or exaggerated?

2. How did the pandemic affect your traditional gatherings? Were there empty chairs at your table due to death or precaution? Was there an empty chair intended for you at someone else's table?

3. What do you do when a guest list isn't shaping up the way you'd hoped? Do you invite more people to fill the space, or downsize your expectations for the party? Would you consider inviting people who are often excluded or overlooked in your community?

4. The sorrow and loneliness that result from loss or social rejection can be an opportunity for introspection. Consider the author's questions on page 68: "How does our grief and sadness, our anger and mourning transform us? How does it reshape us, from the empty expected responses that may try to fill those spaces left empty in our lives?"

5. Imagine arriving at a banquet and finding that your fellow guests are not the sort of people you expected. How would you feel? Do you imagine God's heavenly banquet might feel this way?

6. Consider this chapter's illustration of a potluck meal with a diverse group of attendees. Does your church draw people from a variety of socioeconomic backgrounds, races, and abilities? If not, why is that? Are they being invited?

Chapter 6

HOSPITALITY AND DISCIPLESHIP

A Meal with Chosen Family

READ: JOHN 12:1–8

There they gave a dinner for him. Martha served, and Lazarus was one of those at the table with him. Mary took a pound of costly perfume made of pure nard, anointed Jesus' feet, and wiped them with her hair. The house was filled with the fragrance of the perfume.

—John 12:2–3

I ONCE HAD AN INTERESTING DEBATE WITH A CATHolic priest about the advantages and disadvantages of being unmarried in ministry. He took the traditional Catholic position that being single frees the priest from family obligations and thus gives him freedom to be fully engaged with the people with whom he ministers. I, who had been unmarried in ministry for many years before getting married, argued for the balance and joy that married life brought me. Loneliness in ministry can be a major issue whether one is married or not, but especially in congregational settings, where family activities are emphasized, being single can be isolating. As a pastor I was blessed that in every congregation I served, there were a handful of individuals and families who opened their lives to me and became like family. Some were my home-away-from-home on those holidays when I could not be with my family members far away. Others would call for a spur-of-the-moment meal at a favorite Mexican restaurant. Whether on special occasions or ordinary evenings, having a table where I was welcomed allowed me to set down the burden and loneliness of ministry and simply rest.

Surely Jesus knew the same need. According to the Gospels, most of the time he was surrounded by people: crowds who gathered to hear him preach and those who crowded in, bringing their own pain or that of their loved ones for his healing touch. Jesus had disciples who traveled with him in his ministry through the villages of Galilee, but he had left his birth family behind in Nazareth. I imagine that he, too, needed people who would just treat him like family.

Here, just before the day we call "Palm Sunday," John gives us a glimpse of Jesus at home with some of his closest friends. The hospitality he receives here is not from elated outsiders or skeptical religious leaders. Here, he is with devoted friends. At first glance, this story looks like the one told by Mark and Matthew of a meal just before his death when an unnamed woman came to anoint Jesus' head in anticipation of his death and burial. But John's story is not only earlier in the week; it is completely different in setting and tone. Here, Jesus is at home with people he knows and loves, people whose lives are deeply intertwined with his, people who know who he really is—and treat him like family.

This dinner is at the home of Lazarus and his sisters Martha and Mary. If we look back, we get a fuller picture of this scene of intimacy set in the context of danger, betrayal, and death. In the Gospel of John, we are introduced to this family in chapter 11: "Now a certain man was ill, Lazarus of Bethany, the village of Mary and her sister Martha" (v. 1). Luke also knows a tradition of these two sisters (cf. Luke 10:38–42), and the roles they play in both stories is strikingly similar. While Martha prepares and serves the meal, Mary takes the role expected of male disciples. In Luke, she sits at the teacher's feet; here, she does what Jesus will soon instruct his (male) disciples to do.

One of the things we notice about the story in John 11 is how often the word love occurs. When the sisters send word to Jesus that Lazarus is ill, they say, "he whom you love is ill" (11:3). Then, when Jesus decides not to go immediately to Bethany, his relationship with them is made clear: "though Jesus loved Martha and her sister and Lazarus" (11:5) he stayed where he was for two days. Finally, when Jesus does arrive and goes with Mary to the tomb where Lazarus has been buried, he begins to weep, and the crowd says, "See how he loved him!" (11:36). These are people with whom Jesus has deep and personal relationships. Their mutual affection is clear. And now this dinner before Jesus enters Jerusalem is made all the more poignant by Jesus' impending death.

This story of an intimate family dinner is pivotal for this part of John's Gospel: it has deep connections both to what has come before and what will come next. The immediate context is the death and raising of Lazarus. Two important things happen in that incident. First, Martha affirms that Jesus is the Son of God, the one who has the power of life over death (v. 27). Second, Jesus' act (or "sign" as John calls it) of bringing Lazarus back from death to life is so threatening to the religious authorities that it sets in motion Jesus' betrayal and death (11:45–53). Lazarus also becomes a target, as the authorities plot to remove the evidence of Jesus' awesome power (12:9–11). Another detail in the dinner story points back to that story as well: as Mary anoints Jesus' feet, "the house was filled with the fragrance of the perfume" (12:3). Gail O'Day writes that Mary's extravagant act replaces "the stench of death that once lingered over this household . . . [with] the fragrance of love and devotion."[1]

1. Gail R. O'Day, "The Gospel of John," *The New Interpreter's Bible, Volume IX* (Nashville: Abingdon Press, 1995), 701.

Other elements of this story anticipate what comes next. Similar versions are found in Mark 14:3–9 and Matthew 26:6–13, where the anointing anticipates Jesus' death: Mary has this perfume "so that she might keep it for the day of my burial" (John 12:7). Unlike the other versions, however, Mary does not anoint Jesus' head but rather anoints his feet and then wipes them with her hair. This action anticipates what Jesus himself does when he and his disciples share their last meal: he takes off his outer robe, girds himself with a towel, and carefully washes the feet of each disciple and wipes them (the same word used to describe Mary's actions) with the towel. There is yet another link between the family meal and the one in the upper room: the word translated "dinner" is the same as the one translated "supper" in 13:2. John wants us to see that deep connection between what Mary does here and what Jesus himself will do just a few days later.

John 13 begins the longest segment of teaching material in the Gospel, often known as the "Farewell Discourse." In these chapters, Jesus imparts a distinctive vision of what it means to be a disciple: "I give you a new commandment, that you love one another. Just as I have loved you, you also should love one another" (13:34). What this love looks like is washing feet: "For I have set you an example, that you also should do as I have done to you" (13:15). With these words, we see now that Mary is the best example of true discipleship. Before Jesus gives the instruction, she knew what to do. Her act of love is a reflection of and response to the love that Jesus has shown to her and her family.

We should pause for a moment and reflect on how radical John's version of discipleship really is. In the other Gospels, Jesus is asked what is the greatest of the commandments. This was a familiar debate among the rabbis, the religious teachers. Regarding all the commands in the Torah as sacred, God's Word, were some "greater" than others? In other words, did some (one or two, perhaps) act as lenses through which to interpret or understand the others? Yes, Jesus said, it is this: "You shall love the Lord your God with all your heart, and with all your soul, and with all your mind, and with all your strength" (Mark 12:30; cf. Deut. 6:4–5).

Then, he added, there is a second that is like the first: "You shall love your neighbor as yourself" (Mark 12:31; cf. Lev. 19:18). Both of these commands are tall orders: to devote oneself entirely to God and to honor, respect, and care for others as you do yourself. That is asking a lot, and it demands a lifetime to put those precepts into practice. But according to John, even that is not enough: "as I have loved you," that is how we are to love one another. Further along in the Farewell Discourse, it becomes even clearer: "This is my commandment, that you love one another as I have loved you. No one has greater love than this, to lay down one's life for one's friends. You are my friends if you do what I command you" (John 15:12–14). The outpouring of Jesus' life is the example to which we are called. Sit with that for a while. Reflect on the enormity of it. If the Word made flesh, the only begotten Son of God, could wash the feet of his friends, who are we to calculate who is worthy of our care or respect?

One of the themes this story invites us to consider is the relationship between hospitality and discipleship. Mary and her sister Martha have welcomed Jesus into their home on multiple occasions. They have been the hosts and he the guest, finding a welcome respite from the press of the crowds and the stress of conflict. But he has also been their host, welcoming them into the company of his followers, sharing with them his message, revealing to them his purpose.

As we draw closer to Christ's final meal, we are invited to consider our practice of the Lord's Supper. In the Reformed understanding, Christ is the host of the meal, and all of us (ministers and members alike) are his guests. How have we been transformed by our practice of coming to his Table? In this supper, Christ offers his very self to us, and we receive him as we eat the bread and share the cup. We pray that having received his body we may then become his body in the world, which surely means (among other things) extending to others the kind of hospitality that he has extended to us. Hospitality is always a two-way street: it transforms all as relationships are formed and life shared. May this be a season in which we discover more deeply what it is to welcome and be welcomed by Christ.

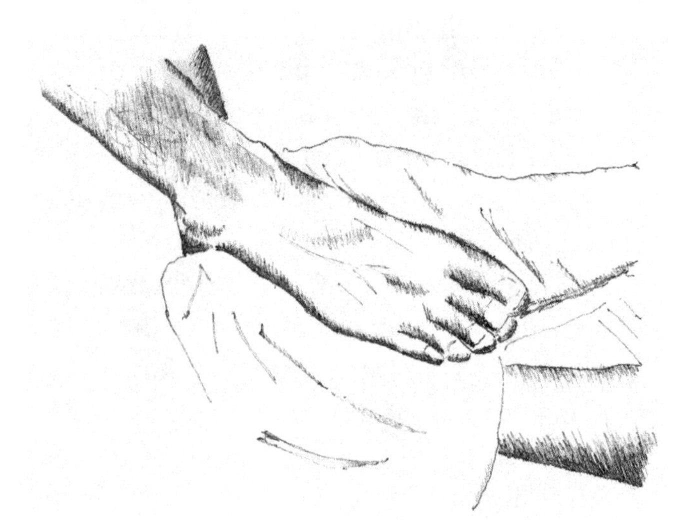

ARTIST'S REFLECTION

Anointed. The term is wrought with meaning. In the Hebrew Bible, it is a reference to being called out and set apart for an important task like being a prophet or king. This type of anointing is usually done with oil applied to the head. The action symbolizes that God's spirit has or will come upon the person. There is an expectation for great things to come. Another type of anointing is preparing the body for burial. When a person dies, family and friends anoint the body with perfumes and oil. This story in John carries both meanings. Jesus is being anointed as the great prophet and king of the Jews, and, simultaneously, the symbolism of preparing the body for death is not lost on the reader.

The Greek word used to describe the outpouring of oil onto the feet in this passage is "*aleiphein*." This word is used nine times in the New Testament. The alternative Greek word for anointing is "*chriein*," which is used for the royal anointing for kingship. This passage is thus communicating a distinctive idea of anointing, and it is worth noting that this same Gospel writer uses the same word when Jesus washes the disciples' feet a few scenes later. This kind of anointing is not about kingship but intimacy. The act of washing or anointing the feet of another is both intimate and humble. In this context, it seems to be an act of compassion or adoration. Jesus seems comfortable being both the giver and receiver of this service. Perhaps he sees this act as symbolic of the community he is trying to encourage among the people he is engaging. Mary is called out for wasting expensive perfume on such superfluous behavior. Jesus seems to be supportive of such symbolic acts when the actions represent such profound meaning.

I decided to focus this illustration on the action focused on the feet. It was my hope that the intimacy and symbolism become the focus, and the perspective of the viewer is drawn to imagine either being the cleanser or the cleansed, the anointer or the anointed, or both. Foot washing is not something most of us find comfortable. There is an intimacy to it that often feels wrong in public settings. Yet this aspect of community is what Jesus was about. He never failed to push his audiences to think about intimacy a little differently. He challenged them to make their communities more authentic and more interconnected.

QUESTIONS FOR REFLECTION

1. Have you ever felt the loneliness of needing a place that feels like home and family? How do you think Jesus felt coming to dinner at his friends' house?

2. What is most compelling to you about this story's relationship to the raising of Lazarus before it and the Last Supper after it?

3. What comes to your mind when you think of "anointing"? What is significant about the Gospel writer choosing the variant of the word that he did?

4. How is hospitality part of your discipleship? Is it an area that comes naturally to you, or one you struggle to engage with?

5. What does it feel like to imagine Jesus hosting you—serving you dinner or washing your feet? How does it compare to thinking of the Communion table as being hosted by Christ?

6. Have you ever washed another person's feet, whether in church or a more ordinary setting? Reflect on this chapter's illustration. How do you feel about washing others' feet and having your own feet washed?

Chapter 7

A MEAL OF MEMORIES

Not the Last Supper

READ: MATTHEW 26:17–30

While they were eating, Jesus took a loaf of bread, and after blessing it he broke it, gave it to the disciples, and said, "Take, eat; this is my body." Then he took a cup, and after giving thanks he gave it to them, saying, "Drink from it, all of you; for this is my blood of the covenant, which is poured out for many for the forgiveness of sins.

—Matthew 26:26–28

One of my family's favorite dinner table stories was about the time we had breakfast in Las Vegas at 5:30 in the morning. We were on the final leg of a driving vacation, having spent the night in St. George, Utah, after visiting Zion National Park. It was so hot in our (sort of) air-conditioned motel, that my grandmother got us all up about 3 a.m. and decreed that we were heading out. No one was sleeping particularly well, so this didn't seem as bad an idea as it might appear. We rolled into Vegas as dawn was breaking over the desert. I worried we wouldn't find anything open, but this was my first visit to a town that never sleeps. There were people playing slot machines while we ate our pancakes nearby. Our somewhat-sheltered Presbyterian family got back in the car an hour or so later and drove home to Pasadena, California, marveling at this small glimpse of a very different world. As we told and retold the story, the heat and fatigue receded into the background. What we remembered was a great adventure in an exotic world.

Meals are one of the favorite settings for sharing stories and memories. Holiday celebrations and weeknight dinners invite conversations that begin: "Remember the time when we . . ." or "Grandma, tell us about when you. . . ." When we gather at tables and rehearse shared memories, we create links between past and future. By telling and retelling our stories, we forge a family identity and pass it on from one generation to the next. For good but sadly sometimes for ill, families and other groups come to know who we are by the stories we tell.

It is not too much to say that Christian identity was formed around the table, in the breaking and sharing of bread, all the while telling the stories of Jesus. When Paul reminds the Corinthians of how they are to conduct themselves at these table gatherings, he quotes what were already traditional words:

> For I received from the Lord what I also handed on to you, that the Lord Jesus on the night when he was betrayed took a loaf of bread, and when he had given thanks, he broke it and said, "This is my body that is for you. Do this in remembrance of me." In the same way he took the cup also, after supper, saying, "This cup is the new covenant in my blood. Do this, as often as you drink it, in remembrance of me." For as often as you eat this bread and drink the cup, you proclaim the Lord's death until he comes. (1 Cor. 11:23–26)

This is the heart of Christian worship, gathering to share bread and cup in remembrance of Christ whose life was poured out and in anticipation that he will come again.

According to Matthew, Mark, and Luke, the

last meal that Jesus shared with his closest followers was a Passover meal—a ritual meal of celebration and remembrance. In Jesus' day, it was one of the three pilgrimage feasts that drew Jews to Jerusalem for a multiday gathering. The purpose was to remember God's mighty act of leading Israel out of slavery into freedom, but for Jesus and friends, the celebration would have been colored by the reality that they lived under the colonial domination of Rome. By the time Matthew's Gospel was written, however, Jerusalem and the Temple had been destroyed by the Romans, and Passover was becoming what it is for Jews today: an in-home celebration retelling the story of God's deliverance even in the face of disasters and defeat.

Of the several versions of this Last Supper, Matthew (and Mark) emphasize how it is infused with the themes of Passover and the exodus. In addition to Jesus' specific instructions to his friends about preparing for the Passover meal itself, Jesus' words over the cup—"this is my blood of the covenant"—recall when Moses sprinkled blood over the people of Israel sealing the covenant at Sinai (Exod. 24:8). And when the meal ends, Matthew says: "when they had sung *the* hymn, they went out" (v. 30, emphasis mine). The hymn referred to is Psalms 113–118, known as the "Great Hallel" (for "hallelujah," literally, "praise the Lord"). This collection was already part of the Passover liturgy in Jesus' day and remains so today. Eventually, Christian preachers and the Gospel writers would focus on Psalm 118 as the source of words with which to describe the mystery of Jesus' mission of suffering, death, and triumph over death.

Memory and anticipation are closely linked. We look back and rehearse stories that ground individual and corporate identity. But that very action allows us to look forward, as we see ourselves not only receiving the stories of the past but also handing them on to those who are coming after us. Jesus shows us this when he says, "I tell you, I will never again drink of this fruit of the vine until that day when I drink it new with you in my Father's kingdom" (v. 29). In some versions, the word "new" is inserted before "covenant" in the words that accompanied the sharing of the cup. Wherever it belongs, this idea of a new or renewed relationship with

God echoes Jeremiah 31:31–33: "The days are surely coming, says the LORD, when I will make a new covenant with the house of Israel. . . . I will put my law within them, and I will write it on their hearts." Even this meal, in the context of betrayal and on the verge of death, looks forward to new and renewed relationship with God.

At the center of this meal, as in all the stories of the feeding of the crowd in the wilderness, are four gestures. Jesus *took bread*. He *blessed it* (or *gave thanks*). He *broke it*, and he *gave it* to them. This simple ritual was (and is) part of any Jewish meal. On the Sabbath as well as other occasions, someone takes bread and says the blessing: "Blessed are you, Lord our God, king of the universe, who brings forth bread from the earth." The one praying breaks the bread and the meal begins. When Jesus took bread and said the blessing, he was doing what he probably did at every meal they shared. This time, however, he adds another layer of meaning: "This is my body." Scholars point out that in Aramaic (the version of Hebrew that Jesus and his companions spoke), there is no word for "body." What

Jesus is really saying is: "This is my *self* which I am giving you, and this is how I will continue to be present with you after I am gone." This is what you are to remember always.

At the heart of this meal is blessing or thanksgiving. This is what Jesus wants us to remember to do: to give thanks. To live lives shaped by words and gestures of gratitude. To know that all that we have and all that we are is a gift from God. Whenever we eat bread, we are to remember that we do not live by bread alone, but by every word that comes from God. And when we eat bread and share a cup in remembrance of Jesus, we are to take in the mystery of God's amazing grace and self-giving love.

The central prayer offered at the Lord's Table in many liturgical traditions is called the Great Thanksgiving because it is an expression of our gratitude for all that God has done for us. Traditionally, that prayer is organized around the three persons of the Trinity. In the first section, we give thanks for God's gift of creation and life itself; for calling us to be God's people, setting us free from slavery, and sending prophets and teachers to help us know God's way. In the second section, we rehearse the story of Jesus, who came among us to show us the full extent of God's love for us and for all. In the third section, we call on the Holy Spirit to make us one with Christ as we share bread and cup and send us out to be Christ's body in the world. There is so much for which to be grateful: life, salvation, and the opportunity to serve others in Christ's name. When this is the centerpiece of our relationship with God, we recognize the truth that our right response to God's abundant grace is deep and abiding gratitude.

The meal we share at the Lord's Table is a remembrance of Jesus' last meal on "the night he was betrayed." This has sometimes led Christians to make this service a somber and almost mournful occasion. While that tone may be appropriate for Maundy Thursday as we reflect on Jesus' impending suffering and death, it is certainly not the tone we should set when the Lord's Supper is celebrated on Easter Sunday. On the day when we celebrate Christ's victory over death, we rejoice that "this *is* the joyful feast of the people of God! People will come from north and south and from east and west to sit at table in the kingdom of God!"[1] As we remember Christ's resurrection, we anticipate sharing the fullness of life with him at the end of time. This is when the words with which Jesus and his friends concluded their Passover are fulfilled:

> The stone that the builders rejected
> has become the chief cornerstone.
> This is the LORD's doing;
> it is marvelous in our eyes.
> This is the day that the LORD has made;
> let us rejoice and be glad in it.
> . . . .
> O give thanks to the LORD, for he is good,
> for his steadfast love endures forever.
> (Psalm 118:22–24, 29)

1. Office of Theology and Worship for the Presbyterian Church (U.S.A.), *Book of Common Worship* (Louisville, KY: Westminster John Knox Press, 2018), 26.

ARTIST'S REFLECTION

The final meal with the disciples before the arrest, trial, and crucifixion is one of the pivotal stories in every Gospel. In three of the Gospels, the story is a Passover meal. In the Matthew version, the story begins with a statement from Jesus, "My time is near" (26:18). In this context, the Greek word used for "time" is *kairos.*

As opposed to *chronos* which refers to the ordinary sequencing of chronological time, *kairos* suggests that Jesus is talking about a time of extreme importance. Matthew's version of the story reminds the reader of the slavery and Passover experience in Hebrew history and implies a reference to the future messianic banquet. This story connects memories of the original Last Supper to future celebrations of both the contemporary church and the emerging community of Matthew's time.

In this story of the original event, there is foreboding of betrayal, rejection, and misunderstanding. There is a cloud hanging over the room as the characters interact. The breaking of the bread forces the reader to imagine the breaking of Jesus' body that is about to happen.

Ironically, equally central to the more modern experiences, is also the breaking of the bread. It is in many ways the most powerful symbol in Christian practice. It represents the universal invitation to the Table. It speaks to hospitality and welcome. It invites us to forgiveness, reconciliation, and understanding of others. For many of us, there is an almost magical moment as the bread is broken in front of us. I chose to focus in on the image of the close-up of bread breaking because the act is so universal and is practiced in so many different contexts. When I watch it performed by a pastor, my eyes are drawn to the moment the bread breaks and the tasty goodness is revealed.

Jesus sets a table of grace that emphasizes second chances, and we celebrate this reality every time we see hands take the loaf and tear it apart. We want to respond by reaching into the warm bread and taking our own piece to satisfy our hunger. This is the moment in Christian practice when we realize again that in the end, the thing that glorifies God is not our belief system or nuanced theology. What glorifies God is how we treat each other, particularly those who don't share our belief system or theology.

QUESTIONS FOR REFLECTION

1. What emotions do you associate with retelling favorite stories around the table with family or friends? What impact do you think this

practice has on the relationships between those around the table?

2. What does it mean to you that Christianity was "formed around the table, in the breaking and sharing of bread, all the while telling the stories of Jesus"? (See p. 97.) In the upper room, the friends were retelling the Passover story, as countless Jews have done over the millennia; what other stories do you think early Christians told over and over while forming their bond as a community?

3. Consider the author's words, "Memory and anticipation are closely linked" (p. 99). How do we "look ahead" while recalling stories from the past?

4. During Communion, does your church use the traditional words of institution from 1 Corinthians 11:23–24 that begin, "On the night he was betrayed"? Does your church use the Great Thanksgiving prayer, which recounts much of the history between God and humanity? What other Jesus stories do you reflect on during Communion?

5. The author explains how the Great Thanksgiving prayer is organized around the three persons of the Trinity, giving thanks for what God has done for us, for the life and death of Christ, and for the work of the Holy Spirit. For what are you most grateful to God? What is most meaningful to you about Christ's ministry? How do you see the Spirit at work in your life and your community?

6. In this chapter's illustration, the artist chose to focus on the specific visual of breaking bread. What specific images from the Last Supper stand out to you?

Chapter 8

EASTER

Revived by the Breaking of Bread

READ: LUKE 24:13–35

As they came near the village to which they were going, he walked ahead as if he were going on. But they urged him strongly, saying, "Stay with us, because it is almost evening and the day is now nearly over." So he went in to stay with them. When he was at the table with them, he took bread, blessed and broke it, and gave it to them.

—Luke 24:28–30

WHEN BOB EBELING WOKE UP THAT MORNING, HE knew this could be a horrible day. The night before had been a cold one—eighteen degrees—and with a morning high of only thirty-six degrees, Ebeling knew the temperatures were cold enough to threaten the plans that had been laid so carefully in the years before. Bob knew that such cold air meant this day could be horrible—*could be*—unless he was able to change their minds.

He called his boss first thing that morning, just as dawn was breaking across the cold night's sky, and told him, with conviction filling every bone of his body, "We have to postpone the launch." He told his boss that those frigid temperatures could have threatened the seals that were designed to keep burning fuel from leaking out and potentially causing an explosion. His boss listened to him and asked him to put the data together. They both knew it would take a lot of convincing to keep that launch grounded.

He spent that morning gathering every shred of evidence that might help those in charge see the tragedy looming if they proceeded as planned. But despite reams of data to prove their case, politics and pressure interfered. And so late that morning, knowing the plan was still a "go," Bob Ebeling and his daughter drove to his company's complex. She remembers her father being distraught and frantic, beating his fist on the dashboard when he told her, "The Challenger is going to blow up." When it did, later that day, she remembers standing beside him as he stood before the TV screen, trembling and weeping loudly.

Soon after that day, Bob Ebeling retired. For many years after, he suffered from deep depression that never seemed to lift. When Howard Berkes of National Public Radio interviewed him on the thirtieth anniversary of the Challenger disaster, Bob Ebeling's words told of thirty years filled with guilt, thirty years of feeling that he had failed to prevent that launch. He said, softly, "I think that was one of the mistakes that God made. He shouldn't have picked me for the job." Mr. Ebeling said that, when he met God one day, he would ask: "Why me? You picked a loser."[1]

On the Emmaus road, those two disciples must have been thinking something similar. It seemed only a few days before that the world had felt so very different. The crowds shouting "Hosanna" and waving palm branches. How quickly it all had gone so wrong. And they—the ones who were his companions—they had

1. https://www.npr.org/sections/thetwo-way/2016/01/28/464744781/30-years-after-disaster-challenger-engineer-still-blames-himself

stood alongside as it all happened. They had witnessed it and somehow failed to stop the disaster that left their friend and teacher dead in a most shameful way. How could they have become so idle and ineffective in those last days? "Why me?" they may have asked themselves. Why would God have picked such losers to call as Jesus' disciples?

And so they walked that long, seven-mile journey from Jerusalem to Emmaus, away from their life of hope and revolution, back to their old ways of catching fish and living, quietly, under Rome's rule. But while they walked and talked, another traveler came alongside them. And he asked them, "What are you two discussing?"—a question apparently so ridiculous it stopped them in their tracks. "What things?" they asked. "The things about Jesus of Nazareth."

When evening came, as these weary disciples came to their lodging for the night, they encouraged their strange traveling companion to join them. And so he did. He sat at table with these despairing friends who, for some reason, had yet to recognize him. But when he took bread and blessed it and broke it, their eyes were opened, and they saw him—Jesus. And just as quickly he vanished from their sight. Overcome, they ran to Jerusalem! They ran that long, full day's journey back to find the disciples so that they could tell them, "Jesus is risen, indeed!"

In his 2016 interview on National Public Radio, Bob Ebeling's words struck a chord. Shortly after the interview, letters started pouring in, filling the mailbox of this 89-year-old man in declining health with assurances that God had *not* made a mistake when placing Ebeling in his position at NASA.

"God didn't pick a loser" one letter read. "He picked Bob Ebeling, a man of integrity who did his job that day."

He received letter after impassioned letter, letters of encouragement and compassion, letters pleading with this man they only knew through the radio to let go of the burden he carried. He heard from two engineers who were also there that day—engineers who had landed on the side of politics and signed off on Challenger's launch. They told him that Challenger was not his burden to bear. And he even heard from NASA, who said that the Challenger disaster is a constant reminder to the agency "to remain vigilant and to listen to people just like him—people who have the courage to speak up."

Three months after Bob Ebeling's initial interview with NPR, he died. His family says that those last three months were like a new life had been offered to him. Because of the kindness and compassion extended to him through letters and comments, he came to see that pivotal day of his life differently. "You helped bring my worrisome mind to ease," he said in an interview just before his death. "You have to have an end to everything."

If we are honest with ourselves, we know that resurrection can be hard to wrap our minds around. It is one of the great stumbling blocks for many people of deep conviction, people who long for the community and thoughtfulness and activism of church but who just can't seem to get over this metaphysical mystery so central to Christian faith. Even for the disciples, who heard Jesus talk constantly about his coming death and resurrection, the concept was absurd. They were slow to believe; they called the women delirious in their talk of resurrection. Even later, as they touched the wounds of the risen Christ, Luke says they still struggled to believe.

But it seems there is something about the table—something about what happens there—that finally allows the resurrection to sink in. That finally allows what was dismissed as an idle tale to be worth sprinting home about.

In an upper room, on the night before his arrest, Jesus said, "This is my body, which is given for you. Do this in remembrance of me." And in the same way, without words even needing to be spoken, he took bread after that long Emmaus journey and broke it. And what happened? They remembered. They remembered it all: all that they had been taught, all that they had been told would happen. They remembered who they were as disciples of the risen one, and they took off to share that good news with any who would hear it.

Resurrection is a power that invites us to remember—to remember what we know, what we have been taught—that truth buried deep within us that, under layers of shame and guilt, can struggle to grow. Resurrection is something we can see and know in this world: a family that stays up all night after a death, keeping memories alive as they share stories and laugh over old jokes. It is the power behind social movements and activism and protest, where people name and claim that injustice and oppression and death will not have the final word but that life exists just on the other side. It is the power of remembering, after long years of denial, one's belovedness. And resurrection is the power behind an 89-year-old man, after years of guilt and worry, finding that burden lifted—if even slightly—in the last months of his life.

When the disciples recognized the risen Christ at table, they remembered what they already knew: that death had not had the final word. And so, they ran to share the good news. And what could have ended with an individual dying on a cross was resurrected into a movement of people called by God to do justice, love kindness, and walk humbly in this world.

We are still witnesses to that movement in which bread is broken and hospitality is extended to all, in which light overcomes darkness and hope sustains us through struggle. May we, therefore, seek to live as resurrection people in this world that knows so much death. May we be resurrection people of hope, of compassion, of justice and, above all, of love.

ARTIST'S REFLECTION

The most developed post-resurrection narrative in the Gospels is this story in Luke of two disciples walking together on the road from Jerusalem to Emmaus. A simple resurrection story wouldn't have required as much detail, but what we get is a developed tale of two disciples talking through the shock of the terrifying experience they had just witnessed and discovering the hope and expectancy of what was to come next. And the revelation comes in the breaking of bread at the shared table.

Key to the story of the "big reveal" is the blindness and lack of recognition that precedes it. Imagine walking in the early morning pre-dawn gray that prohibits seeing detail. There is a grayness everywhere. People are mere shadows and as the sun rises on the horizon, the shadows become darker. This lack of seeing is highly symbolic. The disciples are grieving and engaged in serious discussion, but unable to recognize what is really happening in their midst. The symbolism is clearly meant to imply an extended blindness and lack of awareness that was typical of the Gospels' accounting of the reaction to Jesus' teachings and significance. The Gospel of Luke depicts Jesus as a great prophet, not unlike Moses, who brings a novel message and amazing compassion that proclaims freedom and provides recovery of sight.

What gives depth to the story and emphasizes the disciples' blindness is the inability of the disciples to reckon with the rejection that

Jesus has experienced in Jerusalem. Jesus had warned of its likelihood and even suggested that Jerusalem is where prophets are killed. (Luke 13:33–34). Yet those who traveled with him were not expecting the violence that Jesus experienced in the crucifixion story. This reality is what sets up the great irony of this story. Expectation after expectation is replaced by a reality that reveals much about the workings of God. God can work through the most severe tragedies. God is always surprising us, even as we hold onto our own expectations and fail to see God at work despite our misunderstandings. This story is such a manifestation of this irony: the pivotal point, the point of revelation, being the familiarity of Jesus breaking bread at table. At that point, all that has been in shadow is now illuminated. This visual reality is what inspired my sketch of the three companions lingering in the shadows until the time was right for the enlightenment.

QUESTIONS FOR REFLECTION

1. Have you ever carried guilt over a matter of years for something you've done or for which you blame yourself? What did it or would it take for you to feel relieved of that guilt?

2. Do you imagine the disciples carried that level of guilt in the days following Jesus' death? For what might they have blamed themselves?

3. Imagine the scene when the risen Jesus breaks bread with the two friends and they suddenly recognize him. What impact do you think that realization would have had on the guilt and grief they carried?

4. The author says, "it seems there is something about the table—something about what happens there—that finally allows the resurrection to sink in" (p. 117). What does the resurrection mean to you? Does the Communion Table remind you of this meaning? If not, what does make the message of resurrection come alive for you?

5. The silhouette style of this chapter's illustration suggests the "pre-dawn gray that prohibits seeing detail" (p. 121) before the "big reveal" when the friends see Jesus clearly. Does the "big reveal" of celebrating Jesus' resurrection help you see him more clearly or know him more intimately? How so?

6. What insight from studying Jesus at table will stay with you as this study ends?

GUIDE FOR CHURCH LEADERS

The stories considered here represent only a part of the rich legacy of stories about and told by Jesus that involve sharing food. As mentioned in this book's introduction, the Gospels were composed nearly two generations after Jesus' ministry. Thus, they are shaped by the teaching, worship, and fellowship practices of the early Christian communities. That is to say, believers had been recognizing Jesus in the breaking and sharing of bread well before the story of the Emmaus road was written down. Central as table gatherings were to Jesus' ministry and the life of the early church, opportunities are ripe for studying *Meeting Jesus at the Table* not just in small group discussions but as a whole congregation, and not just during Lent, but at any time of year. Consider the following ways in which to expand on this study and bring Jesus' mealtime teachings to life for your church and community.

SERMON SERIES

Consider the chapters in this book your sermon prompts as you reflect on these Scriptures and develop your messages for the series. For your deeper exegetical work, consider the insightful commentaries found in the *Feasting on the Gospels* series. Most of the passages presented here occur in the Revised Common Lectionary (RCL), and good commentaries can be found in lectionary-based resources such as *Feasting on the Word* and *Connections: A Lectionary Commentary for Preaching and Worship.*

Mark 6:30–44	Proper 11, Year B
Matthew 9:9–13	Proper 5, Year A
Luke 7:36–50	Proper 6, Year C
Luke 14:1–14	Proper 17, Year C
John 12:1–8	Lent 5, Year C
Luke 24:13–35	Easter 3, Year A (and Easter Evening, Years A, B, C)

The exceptions are Luke 14:15–24 (Matthew's *very* different version of that same parable was selected for the RCL instead) and Matthew 26:17–30 (the story of the Last Supper is only read as part of the Passion narrative, thus the best resources would be in a commentary on Matthew).

These are only some of the passages in the Bible that deal with eating and feasting, of course. A useful exercise would be to read through the Gospels and note how many stories make reference to bread (or wine) and dining together. Other passages (notably Acts 3:43–47 and 1 Corinthians 11:17–26) are windows onto the practice of the Lord's Supper (or "breaking of the bread") in the earliest church.

The Old Testament is also critically important to these themes and practices in Jesus' ministry. In considering a sermon series, one might consider how the first readings from the lectionary (especially when these are "complementary" readings) shed light on the Gospel. Alternatively, one could construct a lectionary using the passages referenced in this study (e.g., Exodus 16, Psalm 23, and Isaiah 25:6–7). Other passages invite reflection on the relationship between food and social justice (Leviticus 19:9–10 and Isaiah 58:9–10).

WORSHIP AND LITURGY

Lectionary-based resources can also be of assistance when planning worship on the texts and themes of this series. Volumes of the *Feasting on the Word Worship Companion* and *Connections Worship Companion* offer prayers and litanies inspired by the lections for each Sunday. The *Glory to God* hymnal has hymn suggestions for each Sunday of the three-year lectionary cycle, as well as scriptural and topical indices of hymns that can extend reflection on texts in worship.

A *Meeting Jesus at the Table* sermon series is a good time to introduce the practice of weekly celebration of the Lord's Supper, if that is not already the custom. The earliest Christian communities broke bread in remembrance of the upper room and remembered the stories of other meals shared by Jesus' first followers when they were at table together. It is not too much to say that the Lord's Supper or Eucharist is in the background each time a story of eating or bread is told. This realization invites us to examine our own practices both of worship and fellowship. The 2018 version of the *Book of Common Worship* includes fifty-five different Great Prayers of Thanksgiving (or Eucharistic Prayers). Also included is an outline for composing a prayer (see BCW, pp. 121–23). After studying the passages to be used for a particular Sunday, worship leaders could write prayers for each week, lifting up themes and images specific to those texts. Suggestions are made as well for incorporating music into the prayer. Using these prayers helps worshipers appreciate that although the

Lord's Supper is rooted in the upper room story, it truly connects to all the moments of the biblical stories and of our own lives.

HOSPITALITY

A *Meeting Jesus at the Table* series is also a good opportunity to examine the congregation's practices of extending hospitality. Many denominations, including the Presbyterian Church (U.S.A.), welcome all believers to the Lord's Table (which has not always been the case[1]). Hospitality at the Table invites us to reflect on other ways that congregations extend hospitality (or do not) and what they might be called to do differently. Perhaps it is time to consider ministry with the unhoused in the community. Perhaps members are being called to sponsor refugees or to work with other immigrants. Perhaps the city needs a LGBTQ+ youth group

1. Even as late as the early 19th century, some Presbyterian churches issued "communion tokens" to members who had been judged by the pastor or elders to be sufficiently "prepared," morally and spiritually, to participate. This practice died out as the understanding of the Lord's Supper shifted from a privilege to be earned to God's gift freely given to all.

where young adults can build community in a safe space. Perhaps hospitality means helping people with diverse points of view discern ways to rediscover common ground. Congregations might sponsor community-wide dinners inviting speakers to explore topics such as the need for affordable housing or access to health care. In many cities, the Islamic community holds iftar dinners during Ramadan that are open to the public as a way to build relationships and mutual understanding.

OUTREACH

Throughout this study, connections have been made between stories from the ministry of Jesus and food justice. Consider pairing *Meeting Jesus at the Table* with a study of food insecurity and sustainable agriculture. Are there "food deserts" in your city, parts of town where people do not have ready access to grocery stores that stock fresh and healthy food? How many children in public schools qualify for free or reduced-price breakfasts and lunches? What are the policies that govern access to supplemental nutrition assistance (formerly known as food stamps) in your state? Do restaurants and grocery stores in your community partner with food banks to make excess food available to those in need? Many congregations support food banks and partner with community organizations focused on feeding the hungry, but often the root causes of hunger are not addressed. A good congregational study could go deeper and consider ways to become advocates for adequate food for all.

We do not live by bread alone; the Word of God is food for believers. And yet, it is Jesus, the living Word, who invites us to meet him at tables where we break bread and eat together. Christian discipleship is about discovering in deeper ways what it means to follow Jesus: to savor the abundance of God's goodness, to recognize our own need to be received by God's redeeming grace, to extend hospitality to all and recognize Christ in the persons of all whom we meet. This study is one way to follow the path. The table is set. Come and eat.

CPSIA information can be obtained
at www.ICGtesting.com
Printed in the USA
LVHW111242091222
734871LV00005B/5